Publisher and Creative Director: Nick Wells
Project Editor: Polly Prior
Picture Research: Emma Chafer and Polly Prior
Art Director: Mike Spender
Layout Design: Jane Ashley
Digital Design and Production: Chris Herbert

Special thanks to: Laura Bulbeck, Emma Chafer, Esme Chapman,
Stephen Feather and Anna Groves

FLAME TREE PUBLISHING
Crabtree Hall, Crabtree Lane
Fulham, London SW6 6TY
United Kingdom
www.flametreepublishing.com

Website for this book: www.flametreepop.com

First published 2013

13 15 17 16 14
1 3 5 7 9 10 8 6 4 2

A CIP record for this book is available from the British Library upon request.

ISBN 978-0-85775-871-2

Printed in China

RITA ORA

UNOFFICIAL

Nadia Cohen
Foreword by Alice Hudson

**FLAME TREE
PUBLISHING**

Contents

Foreword

I first observed Rita Ora work her performer's magic more than six years ago. It was during an evening spent mindlessly in front of the telly at home, watching a DVD of little-known Brit flick *Spivs* (2004). Among those acting in the low-budget Cockney crime caper was a fresh-faced, pretty young girl with large, expressive eyes and a mass of curly brunette locks. Playing the part of Rosanna, an Albanian refugee, the competent performance given by the unknown kid actress was one of the few aspects of the film to make a lasting impression on me.

Fast forward to 2012. Bottle-blonde, red-lipped bombshell Rita Ora – and her catchy tunes – are everywhere. I must admit, I didn't recognise her as Rosanna from *Spivs,* but then again, the transformation *is* extreme. All grown up and sporting a drastically different look, the tween actress had somehow sidestepped neatly into the notoriously tough music biz and was making waves as a chart-topping style icon. Her reward? A debut album that quickly turned as aggressively platinum as the shade of her hair.

Ora is someone accustomed to big changes, after all. The star was just a toddler when she and her parents were forced to flee war-ravaged Yugoslavia, settling in the leafy, West London suburb of Ladbroke Grove. Did this early experience shape her? Perhaps. What's certain about Ora is she's got bags of raw talent, a strong voice and a fearless attitude. No wonder she attracted the attention of star maker Jay-Z, who signed her to his label, Roc Nation. Rita's now living her ultimate dream. Yet the greatest thing – both for her fans and the singer herself – is that this may only be the beginning. Young, talented, beautiful and successful, with a gorgeous personality to boot, Rita Ora, you're amazing! I hope you 'Shine Ya Light' on the world with your music for many years to come.

Alice Hudson

Party Girl

Born 26 November 1990, singer Rita Sahatçiu Ora has achieved staggering success in her short career. She blasted into the British pop industry, seemingly out of nowhere, having been spotted by music legend Jay-Z. After her debut album smashed the charts at No. 1, she became the artist with the most No. 1 singles in 2012 and received three Brit Awards nominations. But where did this pop sensation spring from?

'You have to think big, you know.'

Rita Ora

Rita Who?

Just three years ago a talent scout from record label Roc Nation spotted Rita singing in London, and she was flown to New York to meet the boss – Jay-Z himself. He was impressed with what he saw and at the age of just 19 Rita landed herself a lucrative record deal, and appeared in videos for rap icons Jay-Z and Drake. From the moment she made a cameo on Jay-Z's video for 'Young Forever', Rita was being compared to Rihanna. And when Rihanna first met Rita she announced: 'I've just met the British me!'

Rita later revealed she had a huge crush on hip-hop artist Drake, although the two are now just close friends. The single they made together featured a guest rap from Tinie Tempah and was the start of very big things to come for Miss Ora.

'I was in so much shock, the only
thing I could do was act smooth.
I shook his hand and went, "Hey."'
Rita Ora on meeting Jay-Z

Jay-Z Works His Magic

Her introduction to Jay-Z's label Roc Nation came out of the blue. As Rita later explained: 'I was in Boots buying contact lens solution and my mobile went off. It was Jay-Z's partner at Roc Nation asking me what I was up to. He asked if I'd been to America and I said "No". Then he said, "I'm putting you on a flight to New York tomorrow."

'I'd never even been to America before.'

Rita Ora on flying to America

to meet Jay-Z and Beyoncé

I practically had a nervous breakdown when I arrived in New York because I was being taken straight to the Roc Nation Christmas party. I was wearing an old T-shirt and leggings. I had barely any make-up on. I was unbelievably nervous, especially when this big crowd parted and I was face to face with Jay-Z. I was so scared.

A few hours later, I was taken to a studio and sat up all night with the two Jays (Jay-Z and his partner Jay Brown) talking about music, playing music. Then it started to feel normal.'

'It was crazy. I'm never going to forget it for the rest of my life. It was like walking into your own dream coming true. I knew this one person could change my life forever.'

Rita Ora on meeting Jay-Z

Best-Friend Bey

Now Rita refers to Jay-Z and his wife, Beyoncé, as 'my family'. She was one of the first to send a gift to the couple's baby Blue Ivy. As well as her huge admiration for Jay-Z, Rita also considers Beyoncé a mentor in the music industry. She says: 'Beyoncé is this massive star, but she's incredibly humble. But it's weird because even though I love her, she's my boss's wife.'

'I am honoured to have Beyoncé in my life ... she is the nicest person on the planet.'

Rita Ora

A Huge Buzz

Rita's debut release was cleverly orchestrated by Roc Nation, who gradually built up the hype around her by releasing a steady stream of videos while Rita worked on her album throughout 2011. The teasers went viral and created a huge buzz around her. When her debut single 'Hot Right Now' was released in early 2012 it went straight to No. 1 in the UK.

Her assault on the American charts was boosted by appearances alongside her superstar boss Jay-Z, who helped promote her first US single 'How We Do (Party)'. She first heard the single when Jay-Z introduced her to the American public during a surprise visit to a New York radio station. Recalling the life-changing moment, Rita said: 'When Jay took me to [radio station] Z100 in NYC to play my single, I was in shock. When I got into the car I cried. Jay was really happy and just said, "We're happening, kid. This is happening, we're doing this together."'

'You know when you've wanted something for so long? You want it so much that it's not possible for it not to happen in your mind? But when it does happen you're not prepared for the actual experience.'

Rita Ora

Friends In All The Right Places

'Hot Right Now' made No. 1 in the UK and sold over 100,000 copies in the first week. She released 'R.I.P.' in May 2012 and it also made No. 1. By the time she released her album. which featured collaborations with will.i.am, Drake and Kanye West, Rita was already a star.

There was no stopping Rita, who proved her A-list credentials when Simon Cowell chose her as a guest judge for the ninth series of *The X Factor*, making her a household name overnight. She was then invited to tour with Coldplay, as a support act on their massive stadium tour.

'Coldplay are fans of all types of music, and the fact that they chose me is such a huge honour. I'm just going to rock it out and do what I do.'

Rita Ora

Coolest Girl On The Planet

Within four short years Ora has gone from Eurovision Song Contest wannabe to one of the coolest girls on the planet. Rita also made British chart history as the vocalist on one of the first-ever drum and bass No. 1 singles, DJ Fresh's 'Hot Right Now', although she usually brushes the accolade aside with typical modesty. 'That was Fresh's triumph,' she says. 'That's incredible for him. He owns that.'

Even when 'Hot Right Now' rocked the British charts, Rita admitted she was still not confident about her talent. 'It might even be all I'm ever any good at. But I am still really, really nervous about it all.' She had no reason to be nervous. Her album, *Ora*, was instantly a huge hit and she returned to her native Kosovo to make the video for her next single 'Shine Ya Light'.

'It's my name but also ora in my language means "time", and it took me so long to do this album. Like three years.'

Rita Ora

'I never forget how lucky I am.
I always try and put positive energy
into something. I have always envisaged
myself to be at the top of my game.
I set my standards high.'

Rita Ora

Radioactive

At the MTV Europe Awards Rita found herself nominated in three categories – 'Best UK Act', 'Best New Artist' and 'Push Artist'. She also appears as a character in the video game *The Sims 3*.

Inevitably, Rita's eight-date UK Radioactive Tour at the start of 2013 was a huge success and meant studio bosses were keen to get her to record a second album. 'I definitely know what I want more and it's pretty straightforward with what I'm trying to say with this second album,' she said. During the tour, she performed the song 'Fair', which would feature on the follow-up album, alongside a single called 'Torn Apart', which she recorded with American rapper Snoop Dogg, who took her to Thailand to make the video.

'[Roc Nation] never told me to be anything other than the person they discovered, which was Rita the singer.'

Rita Ora

Shining Light

Rita is the second daughter of Vera and Besnik Sahatçiu, born in war-torn Kosovo at the start of the 1990s. As living conditions worsened the family decamped to London shortly before Rita's first birthday, and her parents tried to protect her from the horrors of her past. 'I wasn't made to feel aware of what we had come from,' she said later. 'But obviously when you grow up you get to learn something of what your parents went through to get you where you are today. I owe them everything.'

'I'm most scared of failing, of disappointing people. That's it.'

Rita Ora

Feel Good Factor

Rita began singing when she was just six years old, putting her favourite poems and rhymes to music. Her talent was spotted immediately, as well as the fact she seemed transported whenever she used her remarkable voice. 'What drew me most to singing was the fact that I could make a noise that made me feel good about myself. It was just about doing something that inspired a reaction,' she said. 'It was about self-esteem, even back then. I made a noise, the reaction was positive. I could sing my feelings. It was a new, exciting way of expressing myself. This brand new communication device. I understood the power of it straight away.'

'I used to go in the bathroom, sing in front of the mirror. I'd close the door and write songs, because my sister used to want to sleep.'

Rita Ora

Making Herself Heard

As she started to develop her strong voice and impressive vocal range as a teenager, Rita began to explore London's music industry by performing in local bars and clubs. Thanks to her creativity and original streak, it was not long before Rita gradually started to make a name for herself, in a notoriously tough world.

Although her family's roots are humble, they worked hard for a better life in London. Her mother is a psychiatrist and her father owns pubs in Kilburn and Notting Hill, where Rita often performed as a teenager. 'I did a bunch of gigs there. And helped behind the bar. I can pull a good pint,' she says.

'Music was an obsession for me. My earliest memory is singing a Celine Dion song with my dad.'

Rita Ora

Family Ties

'My dad wanted me to go down a more academic route. He is very much about sticking to the rulebook and sticking to the blueprint of a successful career. So he was wary of my decision. Music is not the most stable nine-to-five job, but it can be the most exciting. It took my dad a while to turn around, but he always, always believed in me.'

Rita remains close to her tight-knit family and her older sister Elena, who still lives in the same three-bedroom flat on a West London council estate where they grew up, now works as Rita's road manager.

'My family has emotionally prepared me.
I don't know what it feels like not to have
a great family support system — I was
lucky to have that.'
Rita Ora

Moving On Up – And Out

It was a rapid rise for Rita, who had shown an early talent for acting and singing and was determined to make a career out of show business, having been inspired by the legendary actress Rita Hayworth. Although she had a strict and fairly traditional Kosovan upbringing, Rita's talent quickly became clear, and her parents agreed to let her audition for drama school.

As soon as she won a place at the prestigious Sylvia Young Theatre School there was no stopping Rita. Former pupils have included Emma Bunton, Denise van Outen and Naomi Campbell, and Rita landed her first movie role in *Spivs* when she was just 14. She had a record deal by the time she was 16 and her first music release when she sang on Craig David's single 'Where's Your Love'. She said: 'This was something I wanted since I was eight. People seem to think this has happened so quickly, but I've been talking to producers and A&R people since I was 14.'

'I listened to different music to everyone else. I wasn't really a musical theatre girl. I was in my own world. I was the one listening to Janis Joplin and choking on a cigarette.'

Rita Ora

Too Young?

At the age of 18 Rita auditioned to be the British contestant for the 2009 Eurovision Song Contest, singing 'Ain't No Sunshine' in front of judge Andrew Lloyd Webber, who was impressed with her talent. Although she sailed through to the final rounds, Rita sabotaged her first major shot at the big time by dramatically withdrawing from the competition, as she did not feel ready. 'I did it because I thought it was a chance to sing, but then I felt inside that it wasn't right for me,' she said later.

'I was incredibly nervous because I was making this really big decision to pull out. Amazingly, the BBC producers were unbelievably kind and supportive, which made me feel more sure of myself artistically. I wasn't going because I had another option, I was going because it wasn't right.' It was clearly the right decision as she hit the ground running with her first album which went straight to No. 1, as did her first three singles 'Hot Right Now', 'How We Do (Party)' and 'R.I.P.'

'I didn't feel like it was right. I thought "if I go down that route, I'm going to have a lot of voices that are going to control me."'

Rita Ora on pulling out of Eurovision

Inspired By Life

Rita's music is inspired by her upbringing in West London where she heard the calypso and raga sounds of the famous Notting Hill Carnival and grew up around the area's rich black music history. 'My first record had to sound exactly like my life,' she said. The catchy 'How We Do (Party)' became an addictive summer anthem and Rita is rightly proud of it. 'I had to learn my pop instinct,' she says. 'The lyrics had to be tough because the song is so immediate. I wanted that twist. This is about the feeling of waking up in the morning and wanting to take another whisky shot.'

'I don't literally take a shot of Jack [Daniels] in the morning. I mean I have once. I have a few times. But it's not like I do it all the time.'

Rita Ora

Keeping It Real

Since she was not the product of a talent or reality show, Rita had credentials with her fans. And it helped that superstar artists lined up to work with her on her debut album, including Diplo, Switch, Stargate, The Dream, as well as Chase, Status and Drake. 'I can't believe how lucky I've been,' she said, 'that these people have even given me the time of day, let alone clicked with me in making my album.'

Rita Loves…

Rita has told how she was also hugely influenced by US megastar Gwen Stefani, not just for her musical talent but also as a style icon. They both share a love for scarlet lips, peroxide hair and out-there designer clothes. Rita once said about the No Doubt singer: 'Do you know how much I love that woman? I love everything about her.'

'I was like: "Hi Gwen, what's up?!" and

we just sat there talking, it was amazing.

I was a bit nervous to meet my idol but

I'm a bigger fan now than I was before.'

Rita Ora on meeting her idol

Gwen Stefani

She is also a huge fan of Beyoncé, whom she credits not only as an influence but also as a mentor. Rita was thrilled when Beyoncé agreed to give feedback on her debut album. Rita said: 'She is the nicest. I call her an alien because I'm like, "How do you do everything at once? You can't be human."' In the same interview Rita also revealed she thinks of Jay-Z as a brother.

Hot Right Now

In April 2013 Hunger TV released two versions of the video for Rita's song 'Facemelt', directed by the iconic photographer Rankin and featuring Rita's best friend, the fashion model Cara Delevingne. Rita and Cara call each other 'wifey', which has led to wild speculation about the true nature of their close relationship. Rita and Cara now hang out with the coolest and most glamorous crowd in London – their circle of friends includes Pixie Geldof, Calvin Harris and Sienna Miller, and when they turn up to parties there is usually some pretty outrageous behaviour to keep the paparazzi happy.

'I found someone who is exactly like me

who isn't really from my world.'

Rita Ora about 'wifey'

Cara Delevingne

Rumours And Romances

Despite the rumours about her sexuality, Rita has been linked to a series of high-profile men including singers Harry Styles and James Arthur, Diana Ross's son Evan, David Beckham's closest friend, Dave Gardner, and singer Bruno Mars, whom she met when they were both unknown and newly signed to their label Roc Nation.

Although Rita rarely talks about the men in her life, claiming 'I'm too busy for relationships' she often talks about her affection for Cara. 'She's officially mine,' she said. 'She's untouchable. I've taken her off the market. We call each other "wifey". You know what a wifey means? It's like your other half. Like when you get married, like, that's your wife!'

The Ritabots

Rita has a huge army of fans, known as Ritabots, who closely scrutinise her every move on social media sites including Twitter, where she has over three million followers, and Facebook where 1.6 million people like her.

Her Twitter row with American rapper Azealia Banks about Cara made front page news on both sides of the Atlantic, as did her bitter break-up with Rob Kardashian. Rob accused Rita of cheating on him 'with like 20 dudes'. In December 2012 – just months after he had described her as 'my wife' – the reality star accused Rita of sleeping with men including her mentor Jay-Z and actor Jonah Hill. After a very public end to her relationship with Rob, Rita seemed to be smitten with Calvin Harris and didn't mind letting the world know they were officially an item.

'All I need in this world of sin is me and my girlfriend @caradelevingne'

Rita Ora tweets about Cara Delevingne

'Nothing matters when u wit the people

you love … #crewdem.'

Rita Ora, Twitter

Super Styling

As well as the partying, Rita is also gaining a name for herself in the fashion world, often praised for her bold style choices. She makes regular appearances at glitzy fashion events and has been tipped to replace Georgia May Jagger as the face of Madonna's Material Girl clothing line.

She is said to have signed a $760,000 deal, and has apparently already shot a campaign for the teen-led line which is sold at US department store Macy's. She is believed to have been recommended by Madonna's daughter Lourdes, 16, who co-designs the collection with her mother.

'I couldn't care less where it's from — it's

just about how you wear it.'

Rita Ora

'When it comes down to the music, it's just you and the microphone. It's not you and the record execs. Some people get mad — you've got to let them get mad.'

Rita Ora

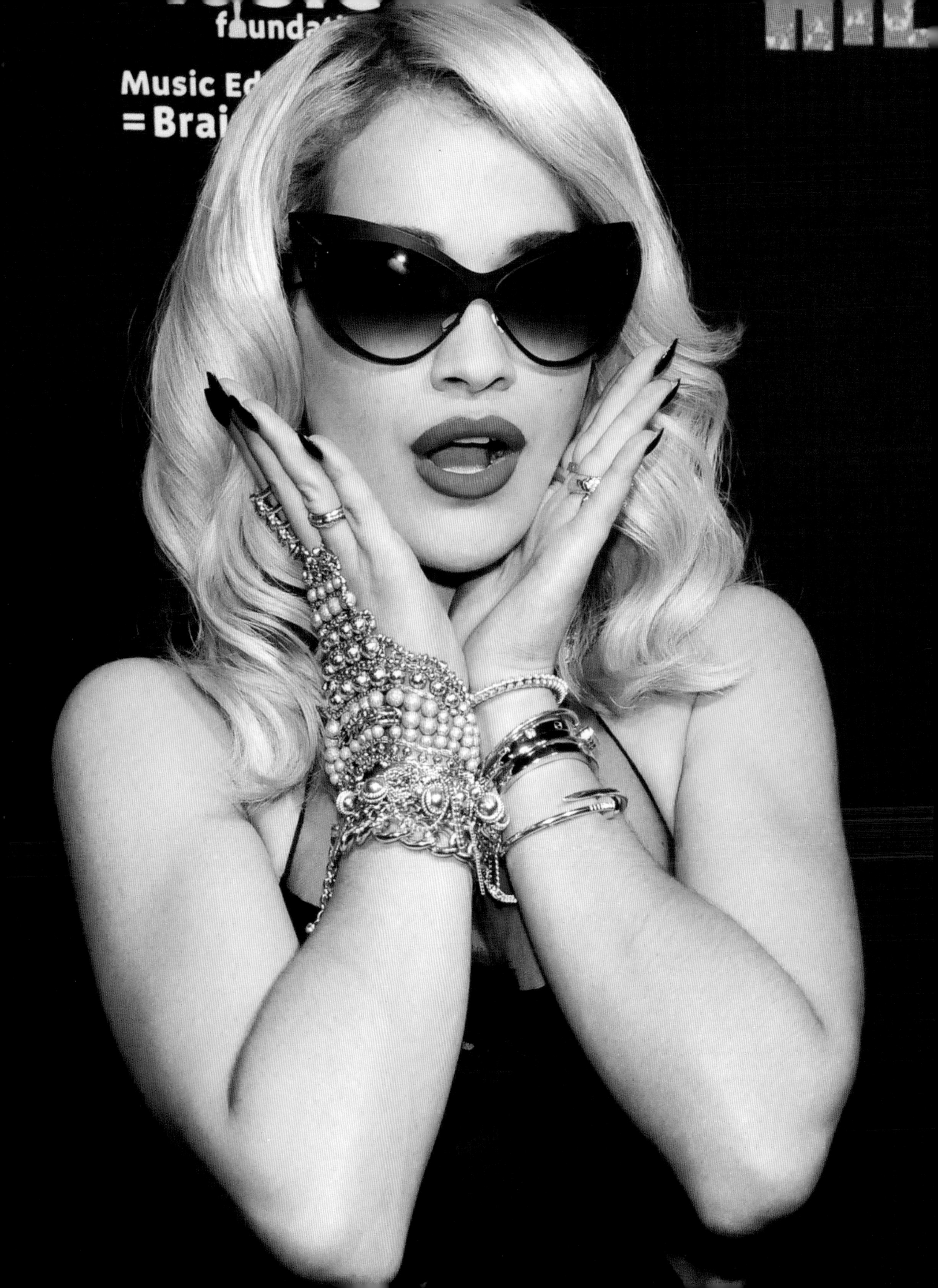

Mixing It Up

Of course Rita is no stranger to the fashion world: signed to Next models, she replaced Alexa Chung as the face of footwear brand Superga and regularly sits in the front row during fashion week events around the world.

She has become legendary for mixing a ball gown with a biker jacket and a pair of trainers from her huge collection. She also mixes cheap costume jewellery with diamonds worth thousands, saying working with a stylist is 'just like playing dressing up with your friends.' Her platinum blonde hair and bright red lipstick have already become trademarks and her look is widely copied by her devoted fans. After one show in London she said: 'They were all rocking red lipstick on the front row! Fierce.'

'Clothes are fun. The designers have so much fun making them, you should have fun wearing them, too.'

Rita Ora

Doing Good

But Rita also has a sensitive side and often works for Unicef in Kosovo – a role she takes very seriously. 'You have such great power and there is so much you can do to influence people to do good,' she said. She is eager to use her fame to put her hometown firmly on the map.

As well as recording the video for 'Shine Ya Light' in Pristina she also played a concert in the city and spoke about how important it is to her: 'I was born in a little city called Pristina which no one really knows about, so I'm proud to kind of put it on the map out there a little bit, because we are a very patriotic country so we always try and mention us wherever we can because it's such a great place.' She added: 'I think [of] Kosovo as a nation – we're very proud of where we're from because it's such a small place, so anyone that succeeds from there is just a big deal.'

'It made everything that I've been doing make sense. I realized how many people are out there who I can inspire and help. I had been inspiring and helping them without even realizing.'

Rita Ora on filming in her native Kosovo

It's Tough Out There

Rita's inspirational charity work counterbalances the tough music industry, which she admits can sometimes be a struggle. She said: 'The music business is brutal but a woman has powers that I don't think a man can ever understand. Not only in a personal way, but also the way that we convey our personalities and I think it's easier for women to connect to people. So it's very much about following your gut instinct as a woman, because it's a manly industry.'

Rita Ora Vital Info

Birth Name	Rita Sahatçiu Ora
Birth Date	26 November 1990
Birth Place	Pristina, Yugoslavia
Nationality	British
Height	166 cm (5 ft 5 in)
Hair Colour	Brown; usually dyed platinum blonde
Eye Colour	Brown

Online

twitter.com/RitaOra:	Follow @RitaOra and join her other followers to see what Rita is tweeting about!
facebook.com/RitaOra:	Head here for all the latest Rita Ora news and check out music videos, tour dates and photos
ritaora.com:	Rita's official website is full of up to date news, videos and music
instagram.com/RitaOra:	Rita LOVES Instagram so go here to check out all of her favorite snaps!
flametreepop.com:	Celebrity, fashion and pop news, with loads of links, downloads and free stuff!

Acknowledgements

Nadia Cohen (Author)

Nadia Cohen is an entertainment journalist who has worked at a number of national newspapers and magazines including *Grazia* and the *Daily Mail*. As a showbusiness correspondent she covered film festivals, premieres and award ceremonies around the world. Nadia was headhunted for the launch of a new American magazine, *In Touch Weekly*, and spent several years living and working in New York. *In Touch* now has a readership of over a million, while Nadia lives in London and juggles family life with showbiz news and gossip.

Alice Hudson (Foreword)

From New Zealand, Alice fused twin passions for writing and music while a student, reviewing and interviewing international bands and DJs. She is currently based in London, writing and researching for corporate clients across a wide range of sectors, from health and fitness and financial services, to social media and entertainment.

Picture Credits

All images © **Getty Images**: Getty Images Entertainment: 1, front cover & 11, 32; Getty Images for BMF Media: 44; Getty Images for DKNY: 36; Getty Images for ELLE: 28; Redferns via Getty Images: 3, 7, 8, 16, 18 & back cover, 23, 24, 26; WireImage: 12, 15, 21, 31, 35, 41, 42, 47.